D0502808

Bus Drivers

By Jacqueline Laks Gorman

Reading consultant: Susan Nations, M.Ed., author/literacy coach/consultant

Gareth Stevens
Publishing

Please visit our Web site www.garethstevens.com. For a free color catalog of all our high-quality books, call toll free 1-800-542-2595 or fax 1-877-542-2596.

Library of Congress Cataloging-in-Publication Data

Gorman, Jacqueline Laks, 1955-
    Bus driver / by Jacqueline Laks Gorman.
       p. cm. — (People in my community)
       Summary: Introduces the work of the bus driver, who helps people
by taking them where they want to go.
      Includes bibliographical references and index.
      ISBN: 978-1-4339-3336-3 (pbk.)
      ISBN: 978-1-4339-3337-0 (6-pack)
      ISBN: 978-1-4339-3335-6 (library binding)
      1. Bus drivers—Juvenile literature. 2. Buses—Juvenile literature.
[1. Bus drivers. 2. Buses. 3. Occupations.] I. Title.
TL232.3G67   2002
388.3'22044'092—dc21
                                              2002024729

New edition published 2010 by
Gareth Stevens Publishing
111 East 14th Street, Suite 349
New York, NY 10003

New text and images this edition copyright © 2010 Gareth Stevens Publishing

Original edition published 2003 by Weekly Reader® Books
An imprint of Gareth Stevens Publishing
Original edition text and images copyright © 2003 Gareth Stevens Publishing

Art direction: Haley Harasymiw, Tammy Gruenewald
Page layout: Michael Flynn, Katherine A. Goedheer
Editorial direction: Kerri O'Donnell, Diane Laska Swanke

Cover, back cover, p. 1 © Anderson Ross/Blend Images/Getty Images; pp. 5, 7, 11, 15, 17, 19, 21 by Gregg Andersen; p. 9 © Shutterstock.com; p. 13 © UpperCut Images/Getty Images.

Printed in the United States of America

CPSIA compliance information: Batch #WW10GS: For further information contact Gareth Stevens, New York, New York at 1-800-542-2595.

Table of Contents

Boldface words appear in the glossary.

Hello, Bus Driver!

A bus driver has an important job. A bus driver helps people.

A bus driver takes people from place to place.

On the Bus

Bus drivers have to drive safely. They must follow all the driving **rules**.

Some bus drivers have the same **route** every day. They stop at the same places.

When the bus driver stops the bus, some **passengers** get off the bus. Other passengers get on the bus.

When passengers get on the bus, they give the bus driver a **fare**.

Off to School

The school bus driver has a special job. He takes children to and from school.

You have to listen to the school bus driver. You have to **behave** on the school bus.

It looks like fun
to be a bus driver!
Would you like to be
a bus driver?

Glossary

behave: to act in a good way

fare: what you pay to ride on a bus or train

passengers: the people who ride with the driver on a bus or train or in a car

route: a path taken from place to place

rule: something that tells what we must or must not do

For More Information

Books

Barraclough, Sue. *Bus Driver.*
  New York: Franklin Watts, 2006.
Frost, Helen. *We Need School Bus Drivers.*
  Mankato, MN: Pebble Books, 2004.
Mitchell, Melanie. *School Bus Drivers.*
  Minneapolis, MN: Lerner Books, 2005.
Owen, Ann. *Taking You Places: A Book About Bus Drivers.*
  Mankato, MN: Picture Window Books, 2003.

Web Sites

People, Occupations, and Community
http://www.enchantedlearning.com/themes/
communityhelpers.shtml

Index

About the Author

Jacqueline Laks Gorman is a writer and editor. She grew up in New York City and began her career working on encyclopedias and other reference books. Since then, she has worked on many different kinds of books. She lives with her husband and children, Colin and Caitlin, in DeKalb, Illinois.